# Living
# From Your Soul

# Living From Your Soul

written by
Karen Katafiasz

illustrated by
R.W. Alley

ONE
CARING
PLACE

Abbey Press

Text © 1997 by Karen Katafiasz
Illustrations © 1997 by St. Meinrad Archabbey
Published by One Caring Place
Abbey Press
St. Meinrad, Indiana  47577

Library of Congress Catalog Number
97-72947


ISBN 0-87029-303-6


Printed in the United States of America

# Foreword

Life is an amazing gift. Yet we can get so caught up in the numbing routine of daily life that we are only half-awake to its depths and riches.

Life is difficult as well. And sometimes when we try to avoid the ache of disturbing feelings, this, too, can numb us from experiencing life to the full.

Occasionally circumstances jar us into deeper awareness—a crisis perhaps, like an illness or a job loss, or a pivotal event, like a birth or a marriage. And then we recognize that we're in the midst of mystery, and—for a moment—we live at a deeper, richer, more intense level.

This is what *Living From Your Soul* is all about—living passionately, mindfully, from your God-graced center. Being wide awake, feeling deeply, knowing what matters, embracing life.

In Thornton Wilder's *Our Town*, the character of Emily asks, "Do any human beings ever realize life while they live it—every, every minute?" She's told: "The saints and poets, maybe—they do some."

*Living From Your Soul* reminds us that there's both saint and poet in each of us. We need only pay attention.

# 1.

Your soul is your deepest, complete essence. It's where God dwells and where you are really you. Be aware of God's presence within you; live out of this awareness.

## 2.

Once you're aware of the amazing reality that God exists at your core, you realize that here within lies your grounding, your foundation, and your compass. You're never alone, and love envelops your heart. Enthusiasm means "God within." You face life with true enthusiasm when you know that God is within.

## 3.

Within your soul, you connect with all that has lasting value. Determine what matters, what has meaning for you. Live out of that meaning.

## 4.

Within your soul, you experience life fully and deeply—its delights, frustrations, joys, challenges, sorrows, losses, surprises, miracles, mysteries. Live out of your soul. Live intensely; live completely.

## 5.

When you live from your soul,
you don't try to numb yourself
from life's sorrows. Nor do you
become so overwhelmed by its
grimness that you stay engulfed
in despair. Instead, face the pain
as you soothe and comfort
yourself in its midst. And then
let it change you, sensitize you,
fill you with compassion.
Know that it will open you
later to deep joy.

# 6.

When you live out of your soul, the spiritual is not just one compartment of your life. The sacred is all of life. Ordinary existence becomes extraordinary. Live this greater reality.

# 7.

You live from your soul through your body. You connect to the world through your skin. Be at one with your body; feel at home in it. Listen to what it can teach you. Use it with exuberance and reverence.

# 8.

Don't deal with life through the intellect alone. You are more than you can think. Experience life fully. Use your senses to experience God's creation in its multiplicity, its variety. Let go into your imagination, your soul to ever deepening truth, ever deepening reality.

## 9.

When you live from your soul,
you touch the souls of others
who have been part of the
human family. Read their
words, view their art, hear
their music. Your own soul
will expand.

# 10.

An external focus is an extraordinarily painful way to live. Constantly asking "How am I doing?" and "Is this what others want from me?" keeps you unsure of yourself, looking outward for approval. Find your validation within.

## 11.

When you live from your soul,
you are the hero of your own
life. Put your energy and
intensity into being you.
No one else can do that as
perfectly as you.

## 12.

Some people will criticize you because of their own perceptions and experiences. They will smash down your spirit because their own spirits have been shattered. You can waste energy resenting them or trying to win them over. Or you can pour out tolerance and let them be. Remember, they need to follow their own soul journey.

# 13.

Trying to meet the world's measures of success is a hollow quest. Be in touch with your own desires and live from your authentic self.

# 14.

When you live from your soul, you're deeply immersed in the moment, the eternal present. It holds within it all the richness of the past and the fullness yet to come. Know that where you are right now is exactly where you should be.

## 15.

When you live from your soul,
you know that the goal of life is
not simply to be safe, secure,
untouched, and untested. Act,
experience, respond to challenge,
and share the love at your center.

## 16.

When you live from your soul, you experience living as learning. From the inside out. Without report cards. Stay aware, and keep growing.

## 17.

Know that it's OK to make mistakes—that's how you learn. Do the best you can—that's the best you can do. Then free yourself by letting go of the outcome.

## 18.

When you live out of your soul, you know that every day is an opportunity for rebirth. You don't have to be bound by the past or your old ways of being. You can start over; you can find renewal. Live a path of transformation.

# 19.

Question, examine, explore, consider, evaluate. Challenge your suppositions—make them your own or revise them and find new realities. Stretch yourself. Have the courage to think new thoughts.

## 20.

Both of these are true: you're valuable and good as you now are, <u>and</u> you can grow and become more than you are. Stay in the dynamic tension of these two realities.

## 21.

Learn about yourself; descend into yourself. You need a deep foundation to build toward the stars. Examine what drives you, what you're trying to feel or not feel. What would make you happy at this moment?

## 22.

What messages did you hear
that now limit your life? What
patterns of behavior, habits, or
compulsions did you learn as
ways to cope that are no longer
effective? You can decide now
how to live your life.

## 23.

If you were wounded as a child, if your needs were neglected or you were shamed or abused, you were left with a hole in your soul. With an awareness of God's love, with self-love, and with unconditional love from others, healing can restore you to wholeness.

## 24.

If you want to live out of your soul, confront the fact of death. Face the reality of endings and no mores and gone forevers. Death tells you that you won't be getting another chance to live this moment again. Death teaches you how to live.

## 25.

Living from your soul means
living with the awareness of
life beyond death, of final
mystery. Live in the midst
of mystery.

## 26.

Life is filled with openings to deeper awareness, to expanded consciousness. Stay open to God's messages, the moments of grace enfolded within events, dreams, other people.

## 27.

Place yourself in the dimensions of infinity and eternity, where there are no boundaries, where there is no end. Seeing the ultimate "big picture" will move you beyond day-to-day struggles to what truly matters.

## 28.

When you live from your soul, personal connections matter profoundly. You need supportive relationships where you and others can reveal your private selves, where you can weather the uncertainties and tragedies of life. Be for one another occasions of grace, of transformation, of redemption.

## 29.

You are co-lover with God. Let love be your driving force, a love that accepts people as flawed but wants them to be the best they can be. Love deeply and without conditions. When you extend your hands, when you open your arms, you free your spirit.

## 30.

Let your soul be stirred by the everyday wonders of living: nature's beauty, a child's smile, the wisdom of your family's oldest member.

## 31.

A great paradox of living: We
are, each of us, utterly alone.
And we are all in this together.
We're interdependent; we're
made for communion. Each
of us is like an angel with one
wing—we can fly only by
embracing each other.

## 32.

When you live from your soul, your work is your path of co-creation with God. Find what delights you; find what matters. Feel the pleasure and deep satisfaction of meeting challenges with confidence and competence.

## 33.

Distractions and busyness can prevent you from living out of your soul, can keep you out of touch with your inner self. Remember that when you extinguish the lights, the stars are the brightest.

# 34.

You can live with dread of
the future and its uncertainties.
Or you can hope and trust and
live in faith that if you find
yourself at the edge of a cliff
with nowhere to turn, God
will teach you to fly.

# 35.

When you lose your sense
of connectedness to God, you
lose your true sense of self.
You feel off-center, unworthy,
insecure. Your spirit is
deadened, robbed of enthusiasm.
Be careful that, from this shaky
center, you don't try to regain
your equilibrium and make
yourself feel better with
misguided or hurtful actions.

# 36.

Turn your life over to God.
Stop trying to control. Life's
experiences will bring you to
an awareness that this is the
choice: you can try to be in
control or you can be at peace.

## 37.

When you keep your life in balance, you're centered in your soul. Include work and play, solitude and companionship, prayer and laughter, exertion and rest in your life.

# 38.

Approach each day as a celebration of living. Joy and inner peace come from entering wholly into the experience of life.

**Karen Katafiasz** is a writer and editor. She is the author or co-author of six other Elf-help Books and *Finding Your Way Through Grief.* She is currently director of communications for the Sisters of St. Benedict of Ferdinand, Indiana.

Illustrator for the Abbey Press Elf-help Books, **R.W. Alley** also illustrates and writes children's books. He lives in Barrington, Rhode Island, with his wife, daughter, and son.

# The Story of the Abbey Press Elves

The engaging figures that populate the Abbey Press "elf-help" line of publications and products first appeared in 1987 on the pages of a small self-help book called *Be-good-to-yourself Therapy*. Shaped by the publishing staff's vision and defined in R.W. Alley's inventive illustrations, they lived out author Cherry Hartman's gentle, self-nurturing advice with charm, poignancy, and humor.

Reader response was so enthusiastic that more Elf-help Books were soon under way, a still-growing series that has inspired a line of related gift products.

The especially endearing character featured in the early books—sporting a cap with a mood-changing candle in its peak—has since been joined by a spirited female elf with flowers in her hair.

These two exuberant, sensitive, resourceful, kindhearted, lovable sprites, along with their lively elfin community, reveal what's truly important as they offer messages of joy and wonder, playfulness and co-creation, wholeness and serenity, the miracle of life and the mystery of God's love.

With wisdom and whimsy, these little creatures with long noses demonstrate the elf-help way to a rich and fulfilling life.

# Elf-help Books

**...adding "a little character" and a lot of help to self-help reading!**

**Living From Your Soul**
#20146          $4.95          ISBN 0-87029-303-6

**Teacher Therapy**
#20145          $4.95          ISBN 0-87029-302-8

**Be-good-to-your-family Therapy**
#20154          $4.95          ISBN 0-87029-300-1

**Stress Therapy**
#20153          $4.95          ISBN 0-87029-301-X

**Making-sense-out-of-suffering Therapy**
#20156          $4.95          ISBN 0-87029-296-X

**Get Well Therapy**
#20157          $4.95          ISBN 0-87029-297-8

**Anger Therapy**
#20127          $4.95          ISBN 0-87029-292-7

**Caregiver Therapy**
#20164          $4.95          ISBN 0-87029-285-4

**Self-esteem Therapy**
#20165          $4.95          ISBN 0-87029-280-3

**Take-charge-of-your-life Therapy**
#20168          $4.95          ISBN 0-87029-271-4

**Work Therapy**
#20166     $4.95     ISBN 0-87029-276-5

**Everyday-courage Therapy**
#20167     $4.95     ISBN 0-87029-274-9

**Peace Therapy**
#20176     $4.95     ISBN 0-87029-273-0

**Friendship Therapy**
#20174     $4.95     ISBN 0-87029-270-6

**Christmas Therapy** (color edition)
#20175     $5.95     ISBN 0-87029-268-4

**Grief Therapy**
#20178     $4.95     ISBN 0-87029-267-6

**More Be-good-to-yourself Therapy**
#20180     $3.95     ISBN 0-87029-262-5

**Happy Birthday Therapy**
#20181     $4.95     ISBN 0-87029-260-9

**Forgiveness Therapy**
#20184     $4.95     ISBN 0-87029-258-7

**Keep-life-simple Therapy**
#20185     $4.95     ISBN 0-87029-257-9

**Be-good-to-your-body Therapy**
#20188     $4.95     ISBN 0-87029-255-2

**Celebrate-your-womanhood Therapy**
#20189     $4.95     ISBN 0-87029-254-4

**Acceptance Therapy** (color edition)
#20182     $5.95     ISBN 0-87029-259-5

**Acceptance Therapy**
#20190      $4.95      ISBN 0-87029-245-5

**Keeping-up-your-spirits Therapy**
#20195      $4.95      ISBN 0-87029-242-0

**Play Therapy**
#20200      $4.95      ISBN 0-87029-233-1

**Slow-down Therapy**
#20203      $4.95      ISBN 0-87029-229-3

**One-day-at-a-time Therapy**
#20204      $4.95      ISBN 0-87029-228-5

**Prayer Therapy**
#20206      $4.95      ISBN 0-87029-225-0

**Be-good-to-your-marriage Therapy**
#20205      $4.95      ISBN 0-87029-224-2

**Be-good-to-yourself Therapy** (hardcover)
#20196      $10.95      ISBN 0-87029-243-9

**Be-good-to-yourself Therapy**
#20255      $4.95      ISBN 0-87029-209-9

Available at your favorite bookstore or directly
from us at: One Caring Place, Abbey Press
Publications, St. Meinrad, IN 47577.
Or call 1-800-325-2511.